fresh food fast

delicious no-fuss healthy recipes

THE AUSTRALIAN Women's Weekly

contents

Wish this book had come around years ago when I, as a working mum, still had my son living at home – at least it's appeared in good time for my daughter-in-law! Most of us can get a fast meal on the table, due to supermarket convenience foods and the corner takeaway, but to ensure that this meal is nutritional and well-balanced isn't quite so easy. With the recipes inside *Fresh Food Fast*, however, it will be – easy, healthy, tasty: every working cook's dream.

Pamela Clark
Food Director

fresh is beautiful

This book came about because we wanted to prove that it *is* possible to come up with uncomplicated yet interesting menu ideas for weeknight dining: that it doesn't have to become a logistical nightmare trying to get a healthy home-cooked meal on the table in less than an hour.

The frantic lifestyle many of us lead, dominated by work, appointments, traffic jams and time-consuming mind-numbing chores, comes at the expense of spending quality time with family and friends. And the last thing you feel like doing when you finally come in the door at night is walking straight to the kitchen to spend yet more time working on a complicated meal that takes ages to get to the table. Cooking becomes just another chore when, in fact, it should be a labour of love, a recreation, pure enjoyment. Plus, at that time of day, you crave something fast, something easy, leaving you with a little time to water the garden, help with homework or just put your feet up and watch the news.

Fast food doesn't have to mean fast-food, that quick pick-up-and-turn-around from a take-away chain. Fast can happen at home, with fresh ingredients, simple yet inspired ideas, and a modicum of organisation and preparedness. To start you on your way, the recipes in this book have all been developed with the number of ingredients and length of preparation time under strict scrutiny, and consideration was given to both the use of natural foods (not packaged products) and cutting back on as much fat as possible.

Simple food is more often than not good food: teaming a grilled fish fillet or lamb chop with a few different steamed vegies allows the native qualities of the food to shine through; there's no need for slow-cooking or slathering them in demandingly difficult sauces. Quality fresh ingredients are crucial so it's worth investing a bit more money into the shopping game-plan: the best ingredients require less cooking time, taste better, don't need much trimming so there's little wastage, and because they are also the freshest, they are more replete with health-giving nutrients.

The benefits to your body from eating healthy food are extremely cleansing and energising, as well as exceptionally nourishing. It's also easier to have a good night's sleep when your system isn't suffering from heavy, greasy, even synthetic, food overload.

Whether cooking for a family of five or just for yourself, following these recipes means you won't start panicking in the kitchen every night after work; easy to prepare, versatile and yummy, too, they are perfect for the cook in a hurry. Being organised means that it won't be an arduous task to prepare a fantastic weeknight meal, and a bit of planning can also inject a sense of pleasure into cooking.

timesavers & tastegrabbers

+ Sit down and plan a week's worth of evening meals. Make out a list of exactly what you need, and shop accordingly. This is a sure way to save time and will avoid unnecessary running around. It will also save you money because you won't be piling items in the trolley that you have no plan to use.

+ Buy your meat from a butcher to ensure superior quality and optimal freshness; to reduce time, select fast-cooking cuts.

+ Load up on seasonal fresh fruit and vegies when they're at their cheapest and their best; have a variety of leafy greens and other vegetables on hand to make a simple, quick salad to accompany your main meal.

+ Introduce your family to the wonderful world of fish and seafood; not only is it good for you, it's just about the quickest meal there is to cook.

snacks

fetta and olive dip with garlic toast

Blend or process ⅓ cup seeded green olives, 200g soft fetta cheese, 1 clove garlic and ¾ cup yogurt until smooth. Place in serving bowl; stir in 2 tablespoons finely chopped green olives. Cut 1 loaf ciabatta into 18 slices. Combine 2 tablespoons olive oil and 2 crushed garlic cloves in small bowl. Brush bread with oil mixture; grill until browned both sides. Halve slices diagonally; serve with dip.

serves 6

per serving 17.9g total fat (7.1g saturated fat); 1668kJ (399 cal); 43.3g carbohydrate; 14.3g protein; 3.1g fibre

prosciutto, fig and goat cheese bites

Cut four figs into quarters. Spread ¼ cup soft goat cheese evenly onto 16 slices prosciutto; place a fig quarter and a few baby rocket leaves on each slice prosciutto. Roll to enclose; secure with toothpick if necessary.

serves 8

per serving 3.4g total fat (1.5g saturated fat); 326kJ (78 cal); 2.7g carbohydrate; 8.9g protein; 0.8g fibre

hot and spicy popcorn

Cook ½ cup popping corn with ⅓ cup vegetable oil in large saucepan, covered, shaking pan occasionally, until corn stops popping; place in large bowl. Add 40g melted butter, 1 teaspoon cayenne pepper, 1 teaspoon paprika and 2 teaspoons sea salt; toss well to combine.

makes 12 cups

per ½ cup 4.6g total fat (1.4g saturated fat); 209kJ (50 cal); 1.7g carbohydrate; 0.4g protein; 0.7g fibre

orange and honey nut mix

Preheat oven to 180°C/160°C fan-forced. Combine 1 cup raw unsalted cashews, 1 cup raw unsalted peanuts, 1 cup raw almond kernels, 1 tablespoon finely grated orange rind and ¼ cup honey in large bowl. Spread mixture onto baking-paper-lined oven tray; cook, stirring occasionally, about 20 minutes or until crunchy. Cool mixture, stirring occasionally to prevent clumping.

makes 3 cups

per ½ cup 35g total fat (4.5g saturated fat); 1885kJ (451 cal); 18.9g carbohydrate; 14.3g protein; 5.3g fibre

smoked salmon bruschetta

Combine 200g crème fraîche, 2 tablespoons rinsed, drained baby capers, 2 teaspoons finely grated lemon rind, 2 teaspoons lemon juice and 2 teaspoons finely chopped fresh dill in small bowl. Cut 1 long baguette into 16 slices; toast, both sides, under preheated grill. Spread with crème fraîche mixture. Divide 200g thinly sliced smoked salmon among toast slices; top each with thinly sliced red onion and dill sprig.

serves 8

per serving 12.5g total fat (6.9g saturated fat); 1012kJ (242 cal); 21.6g carbohydrate; 9.9g protein; 1.6g fibre

hot and spicy popcorn

fetta and olive dip with garlic toast

prosciutto, fig and goat cheese bites

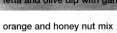
orange and honey nut mix

smoked salmon bruschetta

seafood

chilli prawn and lime risotto

preparation time 10 minutes
cooking time 35 minutes
serves 4
per serving 8.6g total fat
(4.8g saturated fat); 2366kJ
(566 cal); 83.7g carbohydrate;
35.7g protein; 1.5g fibre

10cm stick fresh lemon grass (20g), halved lengthways
1 litre (4 cups) chicken stock
1½ cups (375ml) water
1 tablespoon finely grated lime rind
½ cup (125ml) lime juice
30g butter
2 cloves garlic, crushed
2 fresh small red thai chillies, chopped finely
2 cups (400g) arborio rice
1kg uncooked medium king prawns
⅓ cup coarsely chopped fresh mint

1 Bruise lemon grass, combine in medium saucepan with stock, the water, rind and juice; bring to a boil. Reduce heat; simmer, covered.

2 Melt butter in large saucepan; cook garlic and chilli, stirring, until fragrant. Add rice; stir to coat in butter mixture. Add 1 cup simmering stock mixture; cook, stirring, over low heat, until stock is absorbed. Continue adding stock mixture, in 1-cup batches, stirring, until absorbed between additions. Total cooking time should be about 25 minutes or until rice is just tender.

3 Meanwhile, shell and devein prawns, leaving tails intact. Discard lemon grass from risotto, add prawns; cook, stirring gently, until prawns are changed in colour. Stir in mint off the heat.

Fresh fish fillets, bought at lunchtime or on the way home, are a stellar example of food that's both good for you and quick to get on the table.

spiced fried fish

preparation time 20 minutes
cooking time 15 minutes
serves 4
per serving 14.8g total fat
(4.2g saturated fat); 1250kJ
(299 cal); 2g carbohydrate;
39.5g protein; 0.1g fibre

We used bream fillets here, but you can use any firm white fish fillet, such as perch, blue eye or ling, if you prefer.

1 tablespoon plain flour
1½ teaspoons ground cumin
1½ teaspoons ground coriander
1 teaspoon sweet smoked paprika
¼ teaspoon cayenne pepper
8 bream fillets (800g)
1 tablespoon olive oil

1 Combine flour and spices in medium bowl; add fish, rub spice mixture all over fish.
2 Heat oil in large frying pan; cook fish, in batches, until browned and cooked as desired.
3 Serve fish with lemon pistachio couscous or potato smash with pea and mint salsa (page 17) and, if desired, wedges of lemon.

serve with

lemon pistachio couscous

Combine 1 cup couscous, ¾ cup boiling water, 2 teaspoons finely grated lemon rind and ¼ cup lemon juice in medium heatproof bowl. Cover; stand about 5 minutes or until liquid is absorbed, fluffing with fork occasionally. Meanwhile, heat small frying pan; dry-fry ½ cup pistachios until fragrant. Remove nuts from pan. Heat 2 teaspoons olive oil in same pan, add 1 crushed clove garlic and 1 finely chopped small red onion; cook, stirring, until onion softens. Stir nuts, onion mixture and ½ cup coarsely chopped fresh mint through couscous.
preparation time 10 minutes cooking time 5 minutes serves 4
per serving 10.6g total fat (1.3g saturated fat); 1321kJ (316 cal);
42.8g carbohydrate; 10.2g protein; 2.8g fibre

baked mussels infused with asian flavours

prawn and scallop chilli jam stir-fry

baked mussels infused with asian-flavours

preparation time 20 minutes
cooking time 20 minutes
serves 4
per serving 1.6g total fat
(0.4g saturated fat); 414kJ
(99 cal); 8.2g carbohydrate;
11.2g protein; 2.1g fibre

1.5kg large black mussels
8cm piece fresh ginger (40g), cut into matchsticks
1 clove garlic, sliced thinly
2 kaffir lime leaves, shredded finely
2 fresh long red chillies, sliced thinly
1 medium carrot (120g), cut into matchsticks
1 medium red capsicum (200g), cut into matchsticks
⅓ cup (80ml) water
¼ cup (60ml) kecap manis
¼ cup (60ml) lime juice
½ cup (40g) bean sprouts
⅔ cup loosely packed fresh coriander leaves

1 Preheat oven to 220°C/200°C fan-forced.
2 Scrub mussels; remove beards. Combine mussels in large baking dish with ginger, garlic, lime leaves, chilli, carrot, capsicum, the water, kecap manis and juice. Cook, covered, about 20 minutes or until mussels open (discard any that do not). Remove from oven; stir in sprouts and coriander.

prawn and scallop chilli jam stir-fry

preparation time 20 minutes
cooking time 20 minutes
serves 4
per serving 14.6g total fat
(2.9g saturated fat); 1513kJ
(362 cal); 16.8g carbohydrate;
38.6g protein; 3.9g fibre

1kg uncooked medium king prawns
2 tablespoons peanut oil
300g scallops, roe removed
2 cloves garlic, crushed
2cm piece fresh ginger (10g), grated
200g green beans, cut into 5cm lengths
350g gai lan, trimmed, chopped coarsely
⅔ cup (190g) prepared thai chilli jam
1½ cups (120g) bean sprouts
½ cup firmly packed thai basil leaves

1 Shell and devein prawns leaving tails intact.
2 Heat half the oil in wok; stir-fry prawns and scallops, in batches, until cooked as desired. Drain on absorbent paper.
3 Heat remaining oil in wok; stir-fry garlic and ginger until fragrant. Add beans and gai lan; stir-fry until gai lan is wilted. Return prawns and scallops to wok with chilli jam; stir-fry 2 minutes.
4 Stir in sprouts and basil off the heat; serve with steamed jasmine rice, if desired.

char-grilled chilli squid and rice noodle salad

preparation time 15 minutes
cooking time 15 minutes
serves 4
per serving 3.1g total fat
(0.8g saturated fat); 1584kJ
(379 cal); 48.3g carbohydrate;
38.1g protein; 2.8g fibre

800g cleaned squid hoods

450g fresh wide rice noodles

1 medium red capsicum (200g), sliced thinly

150g snow peas, trimmed, halved

1 lebanese cucumber (130g), seeded, sliced thinly

1 small red onion (100g), sliced thinly

1 cup loosely packed fresh coriander leaves

⅓ cup coarsely chopped fresh mint

sweet chilli dressing

½ cup (125ml) water

⅓ cup (75g) caster sugar

1 tablespoon white vinegar

2 fresh small red thai chillies, chopped finely

1 Cut squid down centre to open out; score the inside in a diagonal pattern. Halve squid lengthways; cut squid into 3cm pieces.

2 Make sweet chilli dressing.

3 Cook squid on heated oiled grill plate (or grill or barbecue), in batches, until tender and browned.

4 Place noodles in large heatproof bowl, cover with boiling water; separate with fork, drain. Combine noodles in large serving bowl with squid, dressing and remaining ingredients.

sweet chilli dressing Stir the water and sugar in small saucepan, over low heat, until sugar dissolves; bring to a boil. Reduce heat; simmer, uncovered, without stirring, about 5 minutes or until syrup thickens slightly. Stir in vinegar and chilli off the heat.

udon and prawn soup   seared ocean trout and potato smash with pea and mint salsa

udon and prawn soup

preparation time 10 minutes
cooking time 20 minutes
serves 4
per serving 1.5g total fat
(0.3g saturated fat); 861kJ
(206 cal); 16.2g carbohydrate;
30.3g protein; 2.3g fibre

3 cups (750ml) fish stock
3 cups (750ml) water
10cm stick fresh lemon grass (20g), chopped coarsely
4 fresh kaffir lime leaves, shredded
8cm piece fresh ginger (40g), sliced thinly
2 fresh small red thai chillies, chopped coarsely
1 tablespoon fish sauce
1kg uncooked medium king prawns
200g fresh udon noodles
230g can sliced bamboo shoots, rinsed, drained
100g fresh shiitake mushrooms, sliced thickly
60g baby spinach leaves

1 Combine stock, the water, lemon grass, lime leaves, ginger, chilli and sauce in large saucepan; bring to a boil. Reduce heat, simmer broth, uncovered, 10 minutes.
2 Meanwhile, shell and devein prawns.
3 Strain broth through sieve into large bowl; discard solids. Return broth to pan with prawns, noodles, bamboo shoots and mushrooms. Simmer, uncovered, about 5 minutes or until prawns are changed in colour and noodles are cooked as desired. Remove from heat; stir in spinach.

seared ocean trout and potato smash with pea and mint salsa

preparation time 20 minutes
cooking time 30 minutes
serves 4
per serving 29.8g total fat
(9.1g saturated fat); 2324kJ
(556 cal); 24.7g carbohydrate;
44.4g protein; 4.6g fibre

¾ cup (90g) frozen peas
⅓ cup coarsely chopped fresh mint
2 tablespoons coarsely chopped fresh basil
2 tablespoons olive oil
2 tablespoons lemon juice
700g baby new potatoes, halved
40g butter
1 tablespoon olive oil, extra
4 x 200g ocean trout fillets

1 Boil, steam or microwave peas until just tender; rinse under cold water, drain. Combine peas in medium bowl with mint, basil, oil and juice.
2 Boil, steam or microwave potato until tender; drain. Using masher, roughly smash potato with butter in large bowl. Cover to keep warm.
3 Meanwhile, heat extra oil in large frying pan; cook fish, uncovered, until browned both sides and cooked as desired. Serve fish with smash and salsa.

almond-crumbed snapper and chips with lemony aïoli

preparation time 10 minutes
cooking time 35 minutes
serves 4
per serving 43g total fat
(6.7g saturated fat); 3616kJ
(865 cal); 41.7g carbohydrate;
73.4g protein; 7g fibre

1kg russet burbank potatoes
1 tablespoon olive oil
¼ cup (20g) finely grated parmesan cheese
1 cup (120g) almond meal
2 eggs
4 x 275g snapper fillets
cooking-oil spray
lemony aïoli
½ cup (150g) mayonnaise
1 teaspoon finely grated lemon rind
2 teaspoons lemon juice
1 clove garlic, crushed

1 Preheat oven to 240°C/220°C fan-forced.

2 Cut unpeeled potatoes into 2cm-thick chips; boil, steam or microwave until just tender. Drain; pat completely dry with absorbent paper. Toss potato in large bowl with olive oil then place, in single layer, on oiled oven tray; roast, uncovered, about 25 minutes or until browned.

3 Meanwhile, combine cheese and almond meal in shallow medium bowl; beat eggs in second shallow medium bowl. Dip fish fillets, one at a time, in egg then almond mixture, to coat both sides. Place fish, in single layer, on oiled oven tray; spray with cooking oil. Cook fish, uncovered, in oven with potato for about 20 minutes or until cooked as desired.

4 Meanwhile, make lemony aïoli by mixing ingredients in small bowl; serve separately to accompany with fish and chips.

fast fish vindaloo

char-grilled octopus salad

fast fish vindaloo

preparation time 10 minutes
cooking time 20 minutes
serves 4
per serving 16.5g total fat
(2.1g saturated fat); 1375kJ
(329 cal); 5.7g carbohydrate;
37.5g protein; 3.7g fibre

2 tablespoons olive oil
4 x 200g blue-eye fillets, skin on
1 large brown onion (200g), sliced thinly
2 cloves garlic, crushed
¼ cup (75g) vindaloo curry paste
1 cup (250ml) water
2 medium tomatoes (300g), chopped coarsely
⅓ cup loosely packed fresh coriander leaves

1 Heat half the oil in large frying pan; cook fish, skin-side down, until browned. Turn; cook other side until browned. Remove from pan.
2 Heat remaining oil in same pan; cook onion and garlic, stirring, until onion softens. Add curry paste; cook, stirring, until fragrant. Add the water and tomato; bring to a boil. Reduce heat; simmer, uncovered, 5 minutes.
3 Return fish to pan; simmer, uncovered, about 5 minutes or until fish is cooked through. Serve vindaloo sprinkled with coriander leaves and, if desired, steamed basmati rice, pappadums and raita.

char-grilled octopus salad

cooking time 20 minutes
preparation time 20 minutes
serves 4
per serving 9.4g total fat
(1.8g saturated fat); 1668kJ
(399 cal); 10.5g carbohydrate;
65.8g protein; 2.2g fibre

1 fresh long red chilli, chopped finely
1 teaspoon finely grated lime rind
1 teaspoon salt
2 tablespoons rice flour
1kg cleaned octopus, quartered
200g mizuna
150g snow peas, sliced thinly
chilli lime dressing
1 fresh small red thai chilli, chopped finely
1 teaspoon finely grated lime rind
2 tablespoons lime juice
1 tablespoon peanut oil
2cm piece fresh ginger (10g), grated

1 Combine chilli, rind, salt and flour in large bowl; add octopus, toss to coat in chilli mixture.
2 Combine ingredients for chilli lime dressing in screw-top jar; shake well.
3 Cook octopus on heated oiled grill plate (or grill or barbecue) about 20 minutes, or until tender.
4 Combine remaining ingredients in large bowl with octopus and dressing.

Fresh spinach and ricotta agnolotti is found in most supermarkets' refrigerated sections. You can substitute ravioli or tortellini for the agnolotti, but none should contain meat or poultry in their filling.

warm lemon-herbed pasta and fresh salmon salad

preparation time 15 minutes
cooking time 20 minutes
serves 4
per serving 33.7g total fat
(10.6g saturated fat); 2428kJ
(581 cal); 26.9g carbohydrate;
39.8g protein; 5.5g fibre

1 cup (120g) frozen peas
170g asparagus, trimmed, chopped coarsely
500g piece salmon fillet
625g spinach and ricotta agnolotti
½ cup fresh flat-leaf parsley leaves
1 tablespoon water
¼ cup (60ml) olive oil
1 teaspoon finely grated lemon rind
¼ cup (60ml) lemon juice

1 Boil, steam or microwave peas and asparagus, separately, until just tender; drain. Rinse under cold water; drain.
2 Cook fish on heated oiled grill plate (or grill or barbecue) until browned both sides and cooked as desired. Place fish in large bowl then, using fork, flake into chunks.
3 Meanwhile, cook pasta in large saucepan of boiling water, uncovered, until just tender; drain. Place in bowl with fish.
4 Combine parsley, the water, oil, rind and juice in small jug; pour into bowl with fish. Add peas and asparagus; toss salad gently to combine.

poultry

chicken and pasta napoletana

preparation time 15 minutes
cooking time 20 minutes
serves 4
per serving 20.5g total fat
(5.8g saturated fat); 2546kJ
(609 cal); 66.3g carbohydrate;
35.9g protein; 5.1g fibre

You need to purchase half
(approximately 500g) a large
barbecued chicken to get the
amount of shredded meat
required for this recipe.

250g cherry tomatoes
1 tablespoon olive oil
375g fettuccine
2 cups (320g) shredded barbecued chicken
⅔ cup (50g) shaved parmesan cheese
50g baby spinach leaves
⅔ cup firmly packed fresh basil leaves
⅓ cup (80ml) lemon juice
1 tablespoon olive oil
2 cloves garlic, crushed

1 Preheat oven to 240°C/220°C fan-forced.
2 Combine tomatoes and oil in shallow medium baking dish; roast, uncovered, about 10 minutes or until tomatoes are softened.
3 Meanwhile, cook pasta in large saucepan of boiling water, uncovered, until just tender; drain.
4 Place tomato mixture and pasta in large bowl with chicken, cheese, spinach and basil; pour combined juice, oil and garlic into bowl. Toss gently to combine.

Shallot is the name often mistakenly describing a long, thin green onion; a true shallot, or eschalot, is a tiny brown-skinned member of the onion family that grows in tight clusters like garlic and is much used in French cooking, especially sauces.

maple-glazed chicken, shallot and kumara skewers

preparation time 15 minutes
cooking time 20 minutes
serves 4
per serving 12.2g total fat
(3.6g saturated fat); 1484kJ
(355 cal); 26.4g carbohydrate;
33.8g protein; 2.7g fibre

1 large kumara (500g), cut into 2cm pieces
660g chicken thigh fillets, cut into 3cm pieces
12 shallots (300g), halved
2 tablespoons maple syrup
1 tablespoon cider vinegar
1 teaspoon dijon mustard

1 Boil, steam or microwave kumara until tender; drain. Thread kumara, chicken and shallot, alternately, onto skewers.
2 Combine syrup, vinegar and mustard in small bowl.
3 Cook skewers on heated oiled grill plate (or grill or barbecue), covered with foil, 10 minutes. Uncover, brush skewers all over with syrup mixture. Turn; cook, brushing occasionally with syrup mixture, about 5 minutes or until chicken is cooked through.
4 Serve skewers with spinach pecan salad.

serve with

spinach pecan salad

Whisk 2 tablespoons maple syrup, 1 tablespoon cider vinegar and 1 teaspoon dijon mustard in large bowl. Add 200g halved yellow grape tomatoes, 1 cup roasted pecan halves, 80g trimmed baby spinach leaves and half a thinly sliced small red onion; toss salad gently to combine.
preparation time 10 minutes serves 4
per serving 22.8g total fat (1.4g saturated fat); 1166kJ (279 cal);
13.1g carbohydrate; 4.2g protein; 4.3g fibre

grilled citrus chicken with orange and pistachio couscous

preparation time 10 minutes
cooking time 15 minutes
serves 4
per serving 18g total fat
(4.4g saturated fat); 3620kJ
(866 cal); 113g carbohydrate;
60.4g protein; 4.3g fibre

3 cloves garlic, crushed
1 tablespoon finely chopped fresh oregano
¼ cup (60ml) lemon juice
½ cup (170g) orange marmalade
2 fresh small red thai chillies, chopped finely
4 chicken breast fillets (800g)
2 cups (500ml) chicken stock
2 cups (400g) couscous
2 medium oranges (480g)
2 green onions, sliced thinly
⅓ cup (45g) roasted unsalted pistachios, chopped coarsely

1 Preheat oven to 200°C/180°C fan-forced. Oil and line oven tray.
2 Combine garlic, oregano, juice, marmalade and chilli in medium bowl; add chicken, turn to coat in mixture. Drain chicken, reserve marmalade mixture; cook chicken on heated oiled grill plate (or grill or barbecue) until browned both sides. Place chicken on oven tray, drizzle with reserved marmalade mixture; cook in oven, uncovered, about 10 minutes or until chicken is cooked through.
3 Meanwhile, bring stock to a boil in medium saucepan. Combine couscous with the stock in large heatproof bowl, cover; stand about 5 minutes or until liquid is absorbed, fluffing with fork occasionally. Segment oranges over couscous; stir in onion and nuts.
4 Serve couscous topped with chicken.

grilled chicken, brie and avocado on ciabatta

preparation time 5 minutes
cooking time 15 minutes
serves 4
per serving 22.6g total fat
(8.3g saturated fat); 1768kJ
(423 cal); 22.9g carbohydrate;
30.6g protein; 2.9g fibre

2 chicken breast fillets (400g)
4 thick slices ciabatta (140g)
⅓ cup (80ml) sweet chilli sauce
50g baby rocket leaves
100g brie, cut into 4 slices
1 small avocado (200g), sliced thinly

1 Halve chicken pieces diagonally; slice through each piece horizontally (you will have 8 pieces). Cook on heated oiled grill plate (or grill or barbecue) until chicken is browned both sides and cooked through.
2 Toast bread, both sides, on same grill plate.
3 Spread half the sauce over toast slices; top with rocket, chicken, cheese then avocado. Drizzle with remaining sauce.

duck, pear and blue cheese salad

preparation time 10 minutes
cooking time 15 minutes
serves 4
per serving 99g total fat
(27.5g saturated fat); 4431kJ
(1060 cal); 8.8g carbohydrate;
33.1g protein; 6.5g fibre

4 duck breast fillets (600g)
1 small red oak lettuce, trimmed
2 witlof (250g), trimmed
1 medium pear (230g), halved, cored, sliced thinly
1 cup (100g) roasted walnuts
150g soft blue cheese, crumbled
red wine vinaigrette
¼ cup (60ml) olive oil
¼ cup (60ml) red wine vinegar
2 teaspoons wholegrain mustard

1 Cook duck, skin-side down, in heated large frying pan about 5 minutes or until skin is browned and crisp. Turn duck; cook about 5 minutes or until cooked as desired. Drain on absorbent paper; slice thinly.
2 Meanwhile, make red wine vinaigrette.
3 Combine duck, lettuce, witlof, pear and nuts in large bowl; drizzle with vinaigrette, sprinkle with cheese.
red wine vinaigrette Place ingredients in screw-top jar; shake well.

grilled chicken, brie and avocado on ciabatta

duck, pear and blue cheese salad

lime and chilli roasted chicken with baby buk choy

preparation time 10 minutes
cooking time 35 minutes
serves 4
per serving 37.4g total fat
(10.5g saturated fat); 2554kJ
(611 cal); 10.3g carbohydrate;
52.5g protein; 4g fibre

3 cloves garlic, crushed
4cm piece fresh ginger (20g), grated
⅓ cup (80ml) hoisin sauce
¼ cup (60ml) light soy sauce
2 tablespoons lime juice
¼ cup (60ml) chinese cooking wine
1 fresh small red thai chilli, chopped finely
12 chicken drumsticks (1.8kg)
1 tablespoon peanut oil
300g baby buk choy, quartered lengthways
¼ cup fresh coriander leaves
1 lime, cut into wedges

1 Preheat oven to 240°C/220°C fan-forced.
2 Combine garlic, ginger, sauces, juice, wine and chilli in large bowl with chicken; toss to coat in chilli lime mixture. Drain chicken; reserve chilli lime mixture. Heat oil in large flameproof baking dish; cook chicken, uncovered, about 5 minutes or until browned all over.
3 Transfer dish to oven; roast chicken, uncovered, 15 minutes. Reduce oven temperature to 220°C/200°C fan-forced; cook, basting frequently with chilli lime mixture, about 15 minutes or until chicken is cooked through.
4 Meanwhile, boil, steam or microwave buk choy until just tender; drain.
5 Divide chicken and buk choy among serving plates; sprinkle with coriander. Serve with lime wedges and, if desired, steamed jasmine rice.

Rocket, mesclun or baby spinach leaves are ideal greens for an easy-to-prepare and timesaving salad: a quick rinse and a minimal trim is all that's required to make them table-ready in a flash.

cashew and parsley-crumbed chicken with rocket salad

preparation time 20 minutes
cooking time 20 minutes
serves 4
per serving 45.1g total fat
(9g saturated fat); 3206kJ
(767 cal); 30.1g carbohydrate;
57.7g protein; 6.1g fibre

¾ cup (115g) roasted unsalted cashews
¾ cup fresh flat-leaf parsley, chopped finely
1 cup (70g) stale breadcrumbs
2 eggs
4 chicken breast fillets (800g)
⅓ cup (50g) plain flour
2 tablespoons olive oil
250g trimmed rocket
250g yellow grape tomatoes, halved
1 medium red capsicum (200g), sliced thinly
mustard vinaigrette
1½ tablespoons olive oil
1 clove garlic, crushed
1 tablespoon white vinegar
2 teaspoons wholegrain mustard

You need to buy a bunch of rocket weighing about 400g for this salad.

1 Preheat oven to 180°C/160°C fan-forced.
2 Blend or process nuts until they resemble a coarse meal; combine in medium shallow bowl with parsley and breadcrumbs. Beat eggs lightly in another medium shallow bowl.
3 Halve chicken pieces diagonally; slice through each piece horizontally. Coat pieces in flour; shake away excess. Dip chicken in egg then in breadcrumb mixture.
4 Heat oil in large frying pan; cook chicken, in batches, until browned both sides. Place chicken on oiled oven tray; cook in oven, uncovered, about 10 minutes or until cooked through.
5 Meanwhile, make mustard vinaigrette. Combine vinaigrette with rocket, tomato and capsicum in large bowl. Toss salad gently then serve with chicken.
mustard vinaigrette Place ingredients in screw-top jar; shake well.

Some of the varieties of fresh wheat noodles sold in supermarkets look very similar to one another, the main difference sometimes being only in width. Singapore noodles are a thinner version of hokkien, about the size of cooked spaghetti.

singapore noodles

preparation time 5 minutes
cooking time 10 minutes
serves 4
per serving 15.5g total fat
(4.6g saturated fat); 1944kJ
(465 cal); 32.7g carbohydrate;
41.9g protein; 3.2g fibre

450g fresh singapore noodles
1 teaspoon peanut oil
1 small brown onion (80g), sliced finely
2 bacon rashers (140g), rind removed, chopped finely
3cm piece fresh ginger (15g), grated
1 tablespoon mild curry powder
3 cups (480g) shredded barbecued chicken
6 green onions, sliced thinly
1½ tablespoons light soy sauce
⅓ cup (80ml) sweet sherry

You need to purchase a large barbecued chicken weighing approximately 900g to get the amount of shredded meat needed for this recipe.

1 Place noodles in large heatproof bowl, cover with boiling water; separate with fork, drain.
2 Heat oil in wok; stir-fry brown onion, bacon and ginger, about 2 minutes or until onion softens and bacon is crisp. Add curry powder; stir-fry until fragrant.
3 Add noodles and remaining ingredients; stir-fry until hot.

beef & veal

open steak sandwich with roasted capsicum and ricotta

preparation time 15 minutes
cooking time 15 minutes
serves 4
per serving 19.3g total fat
(7.6g saturated fat); 1793kJ
(429 cal); 25g carbohydrate;
36.8g protein; 3.9g fibre

2 medium red capsicums (400g)

¾ cup (180g) ricotta cheese

2 tablespoons coarsely chopped fresh chervil

2 teaspoons lemon juice

4 x 125g minute steaks

1 tablespoon cracked black pepper

4 slices rye sourdough bread (180g)

1 tablespoon olive oil

2 cloves garlic, crushed

40g baby rocket leaves

1 Preheat grill.

2 Quarter capsicums; discard seeds and membranes. Roast under grill, skin-side up, until skin blisters and blackens. Cover capsicum pieces in plastic or paper 5 minutes; peel away skin.

3 Meanwhile, combine cheese, chervil and juice in small bowl.

4 Sprinkle steaks both sides with pepper; cook on heated oiled grill plate (or grill or barbecue) until cooked as desired.

5 Brush one side of each bread slice with combined oil and garlic; toast both sides under grill. Spread bread with cheese mixture; top with capsicum, beef then rocket.

veal cutlets with green olive salsa

preparation time 20 minutes
cooking time 15 minutes
serves 4
per serving 16.3g total fat
(2.7g saturated fat); 1112kJ
(266 cal); 5.8g carbohydrate;
23.4g protein; 1.2g fibre

2 tablespoons olive oil

2 cloves garlic, crushed

1 tablespoon finely chopped fresh oregano

2 teaspoons finely grated lemon rind

1 tablespoon lemon juice

4 x 125g veal cutlets

green olive salsa

1 tablespoon lemon juice

¼ cup coarsely chopped fresh flat-leaf parsley

½ cup (80g) finely chopped large green olives

1 small green capsicum (150g), chopped finely

1 tablespoon olive oil

1 clove garlic, crushed

1 tablespoon finely chopped fresh oregano

1 Make green olive salsa.

2 Combine oil, garlic, oregano, rind and juice in small bowl; brush mixture over veal. Cook veal on heated oiled grill plate (or grill or barbecue) until browned both sides and cooked as desired.

3 Serve veal with salsa and barbecued kipflers or crushed potato (page 78).

green olive salsa Combine ingredients in small bowl.

serve with

barbecued kipflers

Boil, steam or microwave 1.5kg kipfler potatoes until tender; drain. Halve potatoes lengthways. Combine ¼ cup fresh thyme leaves, 1 tablespoon coarsely grated lemon rind, 2 cloves crushed garlic, ⅓ cup olive oil, ¼ cup lemon juice and potato in large bowl; toss to coat in thyme mixture. Cook potato on heated oiled grill plate (or grill or barbecue) about 15 minutes or until browned.

preparation time 5 minutes cooking time 30 minutes serves 4
per serving 18.7g total fat (2.6g saturated fat); 1785kJ (427 cal);
50.1g carbohydrate; 9.2g protein; 7.9g fibre

beef burger with grilled eggplant and rocket

veal scaloppine with salsa verde

chilli and honey barbecued steak

preparation time 15 minutes

cooking time 10 minutes

serves 4

per serving 12.1g total fat
(5g saturated fat); 1354kJ
(324 cal); 11.7g carbohydrate;
42.4g protein; 0.3g fibre

2 tablespoons barbecue sauce

1 tablespoon worcestershire sauce

1 tablespoon honey

1 fresh long red chilli, chopped finely

1 clove garlic, crushed

4 x 200g new-york cut steaks

1 Combine sauces, honey, chilli and garlic in large bowl; add beef, turn
to coat in honey mixture.

2 Cook beef on heated oiled grill plate (or grill or barbecue) until browned
both sides and cooked as desired.

3 Serve steaks with coleslaw or warm potato salad (page 35).

serve with

coleslaw

Place 2 tablespoons mayonnaise and 1 tablespoon white wine vinegar in
screw-top jar; shake well. Place dressing in large bowl with 2 cups finely
shredded white cabbage, 1 cup finely shredded red cabbage, 1 coarsely
grated medium carrot and 3 thinly sliced green onions; toss gently.

preparation time 15 minutes serves 4

per serving 3.1g total fat (0.4g saturated fat); 251kJ (60 cal);

4.9g carbohydrate; 1.6g protein; 3.3g fibre

grilled scotch fillet with white bean and spinach salad

preparation time 15 minutes
cooking time 35 minutes
serves 4
per serving 14.8g total fat
(5.5g saturated fat); 1471kJ
(352 cal); 5.5g carbohydrate;
46.7g protein; 4.3g fibre

4 x 200g scotch fillet steaks
1 clove garlic, crushed
2cm piece fresh ginger (10g), grated
⅓ cup (80ml) lime juice
2 teaspoons sesame oil
¼ cup fresh mint leaves
2 x 420g cans white beans, rinsed, drained
100g baby spinach leaves
1 small red onion (100g), sliced thinly

Many varieties of already cooked white beans are available canned, among them cannellini, butter and haricot; any of these is suitable for this recipe.

1 Cook steaks on heated oiled grill plate (or grill or barbecue) until browned both sides and cooked as desired; stand 5 minutes.
2 Meanwhile, combine garlic, ginger, juice and oil in screw-top jar; shake well.
3 Combine mint, beans, spinach, onion and dressing in large bowl.
4 Serve steaks with white bean and spinach salad; accompany with chilli jam, if desired.

serve with

chilli jam

Combine 2 coarsely chopped medium tomatoes, 2 tablespoons water, 1 tablespoon brown sugar, ¼ cup sweet chilli sauce and 1 finely chopped fresh long red chilli in medium saucepan; bring to a boil. Reduce heat; simmer, uncovered, about 20 minutes or until jam thickens. Remove from heat; cool 5 minutes. Stir in 2 tablespoons coarsely chopped fresh coriander.
preparation time 5 minutes cooking time 20 minutes makes 1 cup
per 1 tablespoon 0.2g total fat (0g saturated fat); 59kJ (14 cal);
2.6g carbohydrate; 0.3g protein; 0.6g fibre

fennel-flavoured veal chops with garlic mustard butter

preparation time 10 minutes
cooking time 15 minutes
serves 4
per serving 29.7g total fat
(13.2g saturated fat); 1831kJ
(438 cal); 2.1g carbohydrate;
39.9g protein; 2.7g fibre

2 teaspoons fennel seeds

1 teaspoon sea salt

½ teaspoon cracked black pepper

2 tablespoons olive oil

4 x 200g veal chops

4 flat mushrooms (320g)

80g butter, softened

1 tablespoon coarsely chopped fresh flat-leaf parsley

1 clove garlic, crushed

1 tablespoon wholegrain mustard

80g baby rocket leaves

1 Using mortar and pestle, crush combined seeds, salt and pepper coarsely; stir in oil. Rub mixture all over veal.

2 Cook veal and mushrooms on heated oiled grill plate (or grill or barbecue) until browned both sides and cooked as desired.

3 Meanwhile, combine butter, parsley, garlic and mustard in small bowl.

4 Divide rocket among serving plates; top each with mushroom, veal then butter.

rump steak in black bean sauce with tangy sprout salad

preparation time 15 minutes
cooking time 10 minutes
serves 4
per serving 15.2g total fat
(5.4g saturated fat); 1547kJ
(370 cal); 19.3g carbohydrate;
37.6g protein; 2.6g fibre

1 tablespoon black bean sauce

1 tablespoon honey

1 fresh long red chilli, chopped finely

3cm piece fresh ginger (15g), grated

600g piece beef rump steak

¼ cup (60ml) lime juice

1 tablespoon peanut oil

2 teaspoons honey, extra

100g snow pea sprouts, trimmed

1 large red capsicum (350g), sliced thinly

1 lebanese cucumber (130g), seeded, sliced thinly

1 Combine sauce, honey, chilli and a third of the ginger in large bowl; add beef, coat all over with mixture.

2 Cook beef on heated oiled grill plate (or grill or barbecue) until browned both sides and cooked as desired. Cover; stand 5 minutes then slice thickly.

3 Meanwhile, whisk remaining ginger with juice, oil and extra honey in large bowl. Add sprouts, capsicum, cucumber and dressing; toss gently to combine. Serve salad with beef.

fennel-flavoured veal chops with garlic mustard butter

rump steak in black bean sauce with tangy sprout salad

lamb

lamb and couscous tabbouleh pockets

preparation time 10 minutes
cooking time 15 minutes
serves 6
per serving 19.2g total fat
(5.4g saturated fat); 2136kJ
(511 cal); 50.9g carbohydrate;
31.1g protein; 4g fibre

⅓ cup (65g) couscous
⅓ cup (80ml) boiling water
2 cups coarsely chopped fresh flat-leaf parsley
2 medium tomatoes (300g), seeded, chopped finely
1 small red onion (100g), chopped finely
1 tablespoon lemon juice
¼ cup (60ml) olive oil
600g lamb mince
1 tablespoon sumac
6 small pitta pockets
½ cup (140g) yogurt

1 To make tabbouleh, combine couscous with the water in medium heatproof bowl, cover; stand about 5 minutes or until water is absorbed, fluffing with fork occasionally. Stir in parsley, tomato, onion, juice and oil.

2 Heat oiled large frying pan; cook lamb and sumac, stirring, until cooked through.

3 Halve pitta pockets crossways; spread yogurt on insides. Sandwich lamb mixture and tabbouleh inside each pocket.

Roasted capsicum is sold in supermarkets and delis, but is easy enough to roast at home the day before you make the mayonnaise. Roast several at once, pack them in oil and store in the fridge.

lamb chops with capsicum mayonnaise

preparation time 5 minutes
cooking time 20 minutes
serves 4
per serving 32.2g total fat
(10.6g saturated fat); 1869kJ
(447 cal); 8.2g carbohydrate;
31.5g protein; 0.5g fibre

If you want to use capsicum you roast yourself, you need about 1 medium-sized red capsicum for the mayonnaise.

100g roasted capsicum
½ cup (150g) whole-egg mayonnaise
8 lamb mid-loin chops (800g)

1 Blend or process capsicum and mayonnaise until smooth.
2 Cook lamb, in batches, on heated lightly oiled grill plate (or grill or barbecue) until browned all over and cooked as desired.
3 Top lamb with capsicum mayonnaise; serve with fetta and olive mash or lemon pistachio couscous (page 10).

serve with

fetta and olive mash
Boil, steam or microwave 1kg coarsely chopped potato until tender; drain. Mash potato in large bowl until smooth with ⅔ cup warmed buttermilk. Stir in 200g crumbled fetta cheese and ½ cup thinly sliced black olives then drizzle with 1 tablespoon olive oil.
preparation time 10 minutes cooking time 20 minutes serves 4
per serving 17.5g total fat (8.9g saturated fat); 1551kJ (371 cal);
35.1g carbohydrate; 16g protein; 3.7g fibre

The crisp, bitey green onion, also known as scallion or spring onion, is often incorrectly called a shallot. It is great eaten raw in a salad or, at most, just cooked briefly as we've done here.

teriyaki lamb with carrot salad

preparation time 20 minutes
cooking time 15 minutes
serves 4
per serving 18.4g total fat
(6.8g saturated fat); 1467kJ
(351 cal); 7.7g carbohydrate;
35g protein; 3.7g fibre

2 tablespoons japanese soy sauce
2 tablespoons mirin
1 teaspoon caster sugar
600g diced lamb
9 green onions
carrot salad
2 medium carrots (240g), cut into matchsticks
1 cup (80g) bean sprouts
1 small red onion (100g), sliced thinly
1 tablespoon toasted sesame seeds
2 teaspoons japanese soy sauce
1 tablespoon mirin
½ teaspoon sugar
2 teaspoons peanut oil

You need to soak 12 bamboo skewers in cold water for about an hour to prevent them from splintering and scorching.

1 Combine sauce, mirin, sugar and lamb in medium bowl.
2 Cut four 3cm-long pieces from trimmed root end of each onion.
3 Thread lamb and onion pieces, alternately, on skewers; cook on heated oiled grill plate (or grill or barbecue), brushing with soy mixture occasionally, until lamb is cooked as desired.
4 Meanwhile, make carrot salad. Serve teriyaki lamb with salad.
carrot salad Combine ingredients in medium bowl.

lamb and pasta niçoise

preparation time 10 minutes
cooking time 20 minutes
serves 4
per serving 29.4g total fat
(8.4g saturated fat); 3219kJ
(770 cal); 76.3g carbohydrate;
45.4g protein; 7.2g fibre

375g penne
¼ cup (60ml) olive oil
600g lamb fillets
4 large tomatoes (880g), chopped coarsely
2 cloves garlic, crushed
1 fresh long red chilli, chopped finely
1 cup (120g) seeded black olives, chopped coarsely
2 tablespoons drained baby capers, rinsed
12 (150g) drained marinated artichoke hearts, quartered
1 cup loosely packed fresh flat-leaf parsley leaves

1 Cook pasta in large saucepan of boiling water, uncovered, until just tender; drain.
2 Meanwhile, heat 1 tablespoon of the oil in large frying pan; cook lamb, in batches, until browned all over and cooked as desired. Stand, covered, 5 minutes; slice thinly.
3 Heat remaining oil in large saucepan; cook tomato, garlic and chilli, stirring, until tomato softens. Stir in olives, capers and artichoke.
4 Return lamb to pan with pasta and parsley; toss gently until heated through.

char siu lamb and noodle stir-fry

preparation time 15 minutes
cooking time 20 minutes
serves 4
per serving 29.2g total fat
(9.6g saturated fat); 2725kJ
(652 cal); 46.6g carbohydrate;
47.1g protein; 8g fibre

2 cloves garlic, crushed
2cm piece fresh ginger (10g), grated
1 tablespoon finely grated orange rind
1 teaspoon sesame oil
750g lamb strips
450g hokkien noodles
2 tablespoons peanut oil
200g sugar snap peas
115g baby corn, halved lengthways
2 fresh long red chillies, sliced thinly
⅓ cup (120g) char siu sauce
2 tablespoons water
1 tablespoon rice wine vinegar

1 Combine garlic, ginger, rind, sesame oil and lamb in medium bowl.
2 Place noodles in large heatproof bowl, cover with boiling water; separate with fork, drain.
3 Heat half the peanut oil in wok; stir-fry peas and corn until just tender. Remove from wok.
4 Heat remaining peanut oil in wok; stir-fry lamb, in batches, until browned all over and cooked as desired. Return peas, corn and lamb to wok with noodles, chilli and combined sauce, water and vinegar; stir-fry until heated through.

lamb and pasta niçoise

char siu lamb and noodle stir-fry

To open a fresh coconut, pierce one of the eyes then roast coconut briefly in a very hot oven only until cracks appear in the shell. Cool then break the coconut apart and grate or flake the firm white flesh.

tandoori lamb cutlets with fresh melon and coconut chutney

preparation time 15 minutes
cooking time 10 minutes
serves 4
per serving 27.3g total fat
(13.5g saturated fat); 1601kJ
(383 cal); 13.2g carbohydrate;
18.9g protein; 5.7g fibre

If fresh coconut is unavailable, use 1 cup finely shredded dried coconut.
The chutney is best if made with a firm (just underripe) honeydew melon.

¼ cup (75g) tandoori paste
¼ cup (70g) yogurt
12 french-trimmed lamb cutlets (600g)
1 cup (110g) coarsely grated fresh coconut
½ large firm honeydew melon (850g), grated coarsely, drained
2 tablespoons finely chopped fresh mint
1 tablespoon lemon juice

1 Combine paste, yogurt and lamb in large bowl; turn to coat in tandoori mixture. Cook lamb on heated oiled grill plate (or grill or barbecue) until browned both sides and cooked as desired.
2 Meanwhile, combine coconut, melon, mint and juice in medium bowl. Serve coconut chutney with lamb and, if desired, pappadums and lemon wedges.

grilled lamb with spicy peach salsa

preparation time 15 minutes
cooking time 10 minutes
serves 4
per serving 17.7g total fat
(8g saturated fat); 1530kJ
(366 cal); 7.4g carbohydrate;
43.1g protein; 1.8g fibre

800g lamb backstraps
spicy peach salsa
1 small red onion (100g), chopped finely
2 large peaches (440g), chopped finely
2 tablespoons finely chopped fresh flat-leaf parsley
1 fresh long red chilli, chopped finely
1 tablespoon malt vinegar

1 Cook lamb on heated oiled grill plate (or grill or barbecue) until cooked as desired. Stand, covered, 10 minutes then slice thinly.

2 Meanwhile, make spicy peach salsa.

3 Serve lamb with salsa and spinach salad or barbecued kipflers (page 44).

spicy peach salsa Combine ingredients in medium bowl; toss gently.

serve with

spinach salad

Place 80g trimmed baby spinach leaves, 1 tablespoon malt vinegar, 2 teaspoons olive oil, ½ teaspoon white sugar, 2 tablespoons roasted pine nuts and 1 tablespoon dried currants in medium bowl; toss to combine.

preparation time 5 minutes serves 4
per serving 7.4g total fat (0.6g saturated fat); 351kJ (84 cal);
2.4g carbohydrate; 1.5g protein; 1.1g fibre

lamb, bocconcini and gremolata stacks

preparation time 15 minutes
cooking time 20 minutes
serves 4
per serving 16.7g total fat
(6.8g saturated fat); 1346kJ
(322 cal); 3.4g carbohydrate;
38.8g protein; 1.2g fibre

4 x 150g lamb leg steaks
1 tablespoon olive oil
1 large red capsicum (350g)
2 tablespoons lemon juice
100g bocconcini, sliced thinly
gremolata
2 teaspoons finely grated lemon rind
2 cloves garlic, chopped finely
2 tablespoons finely chopped fresh basil

1 Preheat grill.

2 Make gremolata.

3 Using meat mallet, gently pound lamb between sheets of plastic wrap until 1cm thick. Heat oil in large frying pan; cook lamb, in batches, until cooked as desired. Place lamb on oven tray.

4 Meanwhile, quarter capsicum, discard seeds and membranes. Roast under grill, skin-side up, until skin blisters and blackens. Cover capsicum pieces in plastic or paper for 5 minutes; peel away skin then slice thickly. Combine capsicum and juice in small bowl.

5 Divide capsicum and bocconcini among lamb steaks; grill about 5 minutes or until cheese melts. Serve stacks sprinkled with gremolata and, if desired, a salad of baby rocket leaves.

gremolata Combine ingredients in small bowl.

pork

noodles and buk choy with mixed garlic mushrooms

preparation time 10 minutes
cooking time 20 minutes
serves 4
per serving 11.5g total fat
(2g saturated fat); 1033kJ
(247 cal); 84.5g carbohydrate;
20.3g protein; 9.2g fibre

600g fresh thin egg noodles
2 tablespoons peanut oil
1 tablespoon finely grated lemon rind
1 teaspoon chilli flakes
2 baby buk choy, leaves separated
¼ cup (60ml) lemon juice
4 cloves garlic, crushed
150g oyster mushrooms, halved
100g fresh shiitake mushrooms, halved
200g swiss brown mushrooms, halved
2 tablespoons kecap manis

1 Place noodles in large heatproof bowl, cover with boiling water; separate noodles with fork, drain.
2 Heat half the oil in wok. Add rind and chilli; stir until fragrant. Add noodles, buk choy and juice; stir-fry until buk choy wilts. Remove from wok; cover to keep warm.
3 Heat remaining oil in wok; cook garlic, stirring, until fragrant. Add mushrooms and kecap manis; stir-fry until mushrooms soften.
4 Serve mushrooms on noodles.

mexican corn and bean stew with tortillas

preparation time 15 minutes
cooking time 15 minutes
serves 4
per serving 9.9g total fat
(1.4g saturated fat); 1935kJ
(463 cal); 70.3g carbohydrate;
16.6g protein; 11.5g fibre

You need 1 fresh corn cob
weighing about 400g for
this recipe.

2 teaspoons olive oil
1 medium green capsicum (200g), sliced thinly
1 medium brown onion (150g), sliced thinly
1 cup (165g) fresh corn kernels
3 medium tomatoes (450g), chopped coarsely
420g can kidney beans, rinsed, drained
1 fresh small red thai chilli, chopped finely
8 corn tortillas, warmed

1 Heat half the oil in large frying pan; cook capsicum, stirring, until just tender. Remove from pan.

2 Heat remaining oil in same pan; cook onion and corn, stirring, until onion softens. Add tomato, beans and chilli; simmer, uncovered, 10 minutes.

3 Stir capsicum into tomato mixture; serve with warm tortillas and either guacamole or coleslaw (page 50).

serve with

guacamole

Mash 1 medium avocado roughly in medium bowl; stir in 1 seeded finely chopped medium tomato, ½ finely chopped small red onion, 1 tablespoon lime juice and 1 tablespoon coarsely chopped fresh coriander.

preparation time 5 minutes serves 4
per serving 7.9g total fat (1.7g saturated fat); 339kJ (81 cal);
1g carbohydrate; 1g protein; 0.8g fibre

zucchini and sumac fritters with tomato and mint salad

preparation time 25 minutes
cooking time 10 minutes
serves 4
per serving 15.6g total fat
(3.4g saturated fat); 1208kJ
(289 cal); 21.7g carbohydrate;
12.8g protein; 5g fibre

6 medium zucchini (700g), grated coarsely
1 medium brown onion (150g), chopped finely
1¼ cups (85g) stale breadcrumbs
3 eggs
2 tablespoons finely chopped fresh oregano
1 teaspoon sumac
2 tablespoons olive oil
3 medium tomatoes (450g), seeded, chopped finely
¼ cup coarsely chopped fresh mint
½ cup (140g) yogurt

1 Squeeze excess liquid from zucchini using absorbent paper until as dry as possible. Combine zucchini in medium bowl with onion, breadcrumbs, eggs, oregano and sumac.
2 Heat oil in large frying pan; drop rounded tablespoons of zucchini mixture, in batches, into pan. Cook until browned both sides and cooked through.
3 Meanwhile, combine tomato and mint in small bowl; serve fritters with tomato and mint salad, accompanied by yogurt.

warm crunchy rice salad

preparation time 15 minutes
cooking time 10 minutes
serves 4
per serving 27.4g total fat
(2.9g saturated fat); 1639kJ
(392 cal); 15.7g carbohydrate;
8.3g protein; 6g fibre

1 cup (200g) wild rice blend
1 medium red capsicum (200g), sliced thinly
1 small red onion (100g), sliced thinly
⅓ cup (50g) sunflower seed kernels
⅓ cup (65g) pepitas
⅓ cup (50g) roasted unsalted cashews
½ cup coarsely chopped fresh flat-leaf parsley
2 tablespoons coarsely chopped fresh oregano
black pepper dressing
1 teaspoon finely grated lemon rind
¼ cup (60ml) lemon juice
2 tablespoons olive oil
1 teaspoon dijon mustard
1 teaspoon cracked black pepper

1 Cook rice in large saucepan of boiling water, uncovered, until just tender; drain. Rinse under warm water; drain.
2 Meanwhile, make black pepper dressing.
3 Combine rice and dressing in large bowl with remaining ingredients.
black pepper dressing Place ingredients in screw-top jar; shake well.

chickpea ratatouille

preparation time 10 minutes
cooking time 25 minutes
serves 4
per serving 10.8g total fat
(1.4g saturated fat); 857kJ
(205 cal); 16.4g carbohydrate;
7.1g protein; 7.7g fibre

2 tablespoons olive oil
1 medium red onion (170g), cut into thin wedges
2 cloves garlic, crushed
1 medium eggplant (300g), chopped coarsely
1 medium red capsicum (200g), chopped coarsely
2 medium zucchini (240g), sliced thickly
400g can chickpeas, rinsed, drained
4 small egg tomatoes (240g), chopped coarsely
2 tablespoons tomato paste
½ cup (125ml) water
⅔ cup loosely packed fresh basil leaves

1 Heat half the oil in large frying pan; cook onion and garlic, stirring, about 5 minutes or until onion softens. Remove from pan.
2 Heat remaining oil in same pan; cook eggplant, capsicum and zucchini, stirring, about 5 minutes or until eggplant is browned lightly.
3 Return onion mixture to pan with chickpeas, tomato, paste and the water; simmer, covered, about 10 minutes or until vegetables soften. Remove from heat; stir in basil.

warm crunchy rice salad

chickpea ratatouille

creamy spinach polenta with roasted vegetables

preparation time 15 minutes
cooking time 20 minutes
serves 4
per serving 19.9g total fat
(7.2g saturated fat); 1856kJ
(443 cal); 43.1g carbohydrate;
19.1g protein; 9.3g fibre

2 medium zucchini (240g), sliced thickly
6 baby eggplants (360g), sliced thickly
4 medium egg tomatoes (300g), quartered
4 flat mushrooms (320g), quartered
2 tablespoons olive oil
2 cloves garlic, crushed
2⅓ cups (580ml) milk
2 cups (500ml) water
1 cup (170g) polenta
½ cup (40g) finely grated parmesan cheese
250g spinach, trimmed, chopped coarsely

You need approximately half a bunch of spinach leaves for this recipe.

1 Preheat oven to 220°C/200°C fan-forced.

2 Combine zucchini, eggplant, tomato, mushrooms, oil and garlic, in single layer, in large shallow baking dish. Roast, uncovered, about 20 minutes or until vegetables are tender.

3 Meanwhile, combine 2 cups of the milk and the water in large saucepan; bring to a boil. Gradually add polenta to liquid, stirring constantly. Reduce heat; simmer, stirring, about 5 minutes or until polenta thickens. Stir in cheese, spinach and remaining milk.

4 Divide vegetables among serving plates; top with polenta. Sprinkle with extra parmesan, if desired.

rigatoni with zucchini, lemon and mint   asparagus and goat cheese risotto

basil-butter kumara patties

preparation time 15 minutes
cooking time 30 minutes
serves 4
per serving 25.9g total fat
(7.9g saturated fat); 1634kJ
(391 cal); 30.9g carbohydrate;
7.2g protein; 4.2g fibre

2 medium kumara (800g), chopped coarsely
40g butter, softened
⅓ cup finely chopped fresh basil
¼ cup (40g) roasted pine nuts
1 clove garlic, crushed
2 tablespoons coarsely grated parmesan cheese
½ cup (35g) stale wholemeal breadcrumbs
2 tablespoons olive oil

1 Boil, steam or microwave kumara until tender; drain.
2 Mash kumara with butter in medium bowl; stir in basil, nuts, garlic, cheese and breadcrumbs. When cool enough to handle, shape kumara mixture into 8 patties.
3 Heat oil in large frying pan; cook patties, in 2 batches, until browned both sides and heated through. Serve patties with tomato and bean salad or guacamole (page 82).

serve with

tomato and bean salad

Combine one small torn green oak leaf lettuce, a 425g can rinsed and drained white beans, 250g halved cherry tomatoes, 100g crumbled fetta cheese, ½ cup loosely packed fresh basil leaves, 1 tablespoon olive oil, 1 tablespoon white wine vinegar and 1 teaspoon dijon mustard in large bowl.
preparation time 10 minutes serves 4
per serving 11.1g total fat (4.5g saturated fat); 690kJ (165 cal);
4.9g carbohydrate; 8.6g protein; 5.8g fibre

roasted beetroot and fetta pizza

preparation time 10 minutes
cooking time 35 minutes
serves 4
per serving 23.5g total fat
(9.3g saturated fat); 2516kJ
(602 cal); 70.4g carbohydrate;
22.5g protein; 12g fibre

2 tablespoons olive oil
1kg raw baby beetroots, trimmed, peeled, quartered
4 cloves garlic, crushed
2 teaspoons fresh thyme leaves
4 large pitta breads (320g)
1 cup (260g) bottled tomato pasta sauce
200g fetta cheese, crumbled
20g baby rocket leaves

1 Preheat oven to 200°C/180°C fan-forced.
2 Combine oil, beetroot, garlic and thyme in medium shallow baking dish. Roast, covered, about 20 minutes or until beetroot is tender.
3 Place pitta on oven trays; spread with pasta sauce. Divide beetroot mixture among pitta; sprinkle with cheese. Cook, uncovered, about 10 minutes or until pitta bases are crisp and topping is heated through. Serve, sprinkled with rocket.

ricotta, basil and pine nut pizza

preparation time 5 minutes
cooking time 15 minutes
serves 4
per serving 16.3g total fat
(5.1g saturated fat); 1760kJ
(421 cal); 50.2g carbohydrate;
16.7g protein; 4.8g fibre

4 large pitta breads (320g)
1 cup (260g) bottled tomato pasta sauce
1 cup (240g) ricotta cheese
¼ cup (40g) roasted pine nuts
1 cup loosely packed fresh basil leaves
50g baby spinach leaves

1 Preheat oven to 220°C/200°C fan-forced.
2 Place pitta on oven trays; spread with pasta sauce. Divide cheese and nuts among pitta. Cook, uncovered, about 10 minutes or until pitta bases are crisp and topping is heated through; serve topped with basil and spinach leaves.

roasted beetroot and fetta pizza

ricotta, basil and pine nut pizza

kumara, rosemary and caramelised onion pizza

preparation time 15 minutes
cooking time 30 minutes
serves 4
per serving 31g total fat
(14.1g saturated fat); 2780kJ
(665 cal); 68.8g carbohydrate;
25g protein; 7.3g fibre

2 tablespoons olive oil

1 large kumara (500g), chopped coarsely

2 cloves garlic, crushed

1 tablespoon finely chopped fresh rosemary

1 teaspoon chilli flakes

40g butter

1 large red onion (300g), sliced thinly

4 large pitta breads (320g)

1 cup (260g) bottled tomato pasta sauce

2 cups (200g) coarsely grated mozzarella cheese

½ cup loosely packed fresh mint leaves

1 Preheat oven to 220°C/200°C fan-forced.

2 Combine oil, kumara, garlic, rosemary and chilli in medium shallow baking dish. Roast, uncovered, about 20 minutes or until kumara is tender.

3 Meanwhile, melt butter in medium frying pan; cook onion, stirring occasionally, about 15 minutes or until caramelised.

4 Place pitta on oven trays; spread with pasta sauce. Divide kumara and onion among pitta; sprinkle with cheese. Cook, uncovered, about 10 minutes or until pitta bases are crisp and topping is heated through; serve sprinkled with mint.

fennel and ricotta pizza

preparation time 10 minutes
cooking time 30 minutes
serves 4
per serving 17.4g total fat
(10g saturated fat); 1827kJ
(437 cal); 51.8g carbohydrate;
15.6g protein; 5.9g fibre

40g butter

2 medium fennel bulbs (600g), sliced thinly

½ teaspoon brown mustard seeds

1 teaspoon finely grated lemon rind

1 tablespoon lemon juice

1 teaspoon thinly sliced orange rind

1 tablespoon orange juice

4 large pitta breads (320g)

1 cup (260g) bottled tomato pasta sauce

1 cup (240g) ricotta cheese

1 Preheat oven to 220°C/200°C fan-forced.

2 Melt butter in large frying-pan, add fennel; cook, stirring occasionally, until tender. Stir in seeds, rinds and juices.

3 Place pitta on oven trays; spread with pasta sauce. Divide fennel mixture among pitta; sprinkle with cheese. Cook, uncovered, about 10 minutes or until pitta bases are crisp and topping is heated through; sprinkle with fennel fronds, if desired.

kumara, rosemary and caramelised onion pizza   fennel and ricotta pizza

desserts

pear, chocolate and almond galette

preparation time 5 minutes
cooking time 15 minutes
serves 4

per serving 19.9g total fat
(11g saturated fat); 1480kJ
(354 cal); 38.4g carbohydrate;
5g protein; 3.5g fibre

80g dark cooking chocolate, chopped finely
¼ cup (30g) almond meal
1 sheet ready-rolled puff pastry
1 tablespoon milk
1 medium pear (230g)
1 tablespoon raw sugar

1 Preheat oven to 220°C/200°C fan-forced. Line oven tray with baking paper.
2 Combine chocolate and 2 tablespoons of the almond meal in small bowl.
3 Cut pastry sheet into quarters; place quarters on tray, prick each with a fork, brush with milk. Divide chocolate mixture onto pastry squares, leaving 2cm border.
4 Peel and core pear; cut into quarters. Cut each pear quarter into thin slices then spread one sliced pear quarter across each pastry square; sprinkle with sugar then remaining almond meal.
5 Bake about 15 minutes or until pastry is golden brown.

Rhubarb is a family favourite that most of us ate as children. Stewed, it can be both the basis for a warming winter dessert such as a crumble, as well as a topping for vanilla ice-cream in summer.

brandy snap and rhubarb stacks

preparation time 10 minutes
cooking time 15 minutes
serves 4
per serving 7g total fat
(4.5g saturated fat); 865kJ
(207 cal); 31.7g carbohydrate;
3g protein; 3.4g fibre

3¼ cups (400g) coarsely chopped rhubarb
2 tablespoons water
¼ cup (55g) caster sugar
30g butter
2 tablespoons brown sugar
1 tablespoon golden syrup
½ teaspoon ground ginger
2 tablespoons plain flour
¼ cup (70g) yogurt

You need about 5 trimmed stems of rhubarb for this recipe. Placing the softened rhubarb in the freezer is to quickly cool the mixture, not freeze it. Cooked frozen rhubarb is available at most supermarkets.

1 Preheat oven to 180°C/160°C fan-forced. Grease two oven trays.
2 Combine rhubarb, the water and caster sugar in medium saucepan; bring to a boil. Reduce heat; simmer, uncovered, stirring occasionally, about 5 minutes or until rhubarb softens. Drain rhubarb mixture through sieve over medium bowl; reserve liquid. Spread rhubarb mixture onto metal tray; cover with foil, place in freezer.
3 Meanwhile, combine butter, brown sugar, syrup and ginger in same cleaned pan; stir over low heat until butter has melted. Remove from heat, stir in flour.
4 Drop level teaspoons of mixture about 6cm apart onto trays. Bake, in oven, about 7 minutes or until brandy snaps bubble and become golden brown; cool on trays for 2 minutes then transfer to wire rack to cool completely.
5 Place cooled rhubarb mixture in small bowl; add yogurt, pull skewer backwards and forwards through rhubarb mixture for marbled effect.
6 Sandwich three brandy snaps with a quarter of the rhubarb mixture; repeat with remaining brandy snaps and rhubarb mixture.
7 Place stacks on serving plates; drizzle with reserved rhubarb liquid.

warm raspberry meringue pots

preparation time 20 minutes
cooking time 45 minutes
serves 4
per serving 0.3g total fat
(0g saturated fat); 1024kJ
(245 cal); 56.3g carbohydrate;
3.6g protein; 4.1g fibre

2 cups (300g) frozen raspberries
2 tablespoons caster sugar
1 teaspoon cornflour
1 tablespoon orange juice
3 egg whites
¾ cup (165g) caster sugar, extra
2 teaspoons cornflour, extra
2 teaspoons white vinegar

1 Preheat oven to 160°C/140°C fan-forced.
2 Combine berries and sugar in small saucepan; stir over low heat until sugar dissolves. Stir in blended cornflour and juice; cook, stirring, until mixture boils and thickens slightly.
3 Blend or process half the berry mixture until smooth. Place in medium bowl then stir in unprocessed berry mixture; divide among four 1-cup (250ml) ovenproof dishes.
4 Beat egg whites in small bowl with electric mixer until soft peaks form. Gradually add extra sugar, beating until sugar dissolves between additions; fold in remaining ingredients.
5 Spoon meringue over berry mixture in dishes; bake, uncovered, about 30 minutes or until meringue is browned lightly. Serve with sponge-finger biscuits, if desired.

banana caramel sundae

preparation time 10 minutes
cooking time 10 minutes
serves 6
per serving 41.7g total fat
(22.4g saturated fat); 2579kJ
(617 cal); 56.1g carbohydrate;
6.9g protein; 2.4g fibre

70g dark eating chocolate, chopped finely
⅔ cup (70g) roasted walnuts, chopped coarsely
1 litre vanilla ice-cream
4 medium bananas (800g), chopped coarsely
caramel sauce
100g butter
½ cup (125ml) cream
½ cup (110g) firmly packed brown sugar

1 Make caramel sauce.
2 Divide one-third of the sauce among six ¾-cup (180ml) glasses; divide half the chocolate, nuts, ice-cream and banana among glasses. Repeat layering process, ending with a layer of the sauce.
caramel sauce Combine ingredients in small saucepan. Stir over low heat until sugar dissolves; bring to a boil. Reduce heat; simmer, uncovered, 5 minutes. Cool.

citrus salad with lime and mint granita

preparation time 15 minutes
serves 4
per serving 0.4g total fat
(0g saturated fat); 385kJ
(92 cal); 18.1g carbohydrate;
2.1g protein; 2.7g fibre

2 medium oranges (480g)
2 small pink grapefruits (700g)
⅓ cup finely chopped fresh mint
2 tablespoons icing sugar
1 tablespoon lime juice
2 cups ice cubes

1 Segment orange and grapefruit into medium bowl.
2 Blend or process mint, sugar, juice and ice until ice is crushed; serve with fruit.

banana caramel sundae

citrus salad with lime and mint granita

Pav without tears on a weeknight! Loads of fresh fruit and crushed meringue marry in this blissfully simple and quick-to-make dessert that fulfils our wistful expectations of a decadent sweet.

pavlova trifle

preparation time 25 minutes
serves 4
per serving 36.9g total fat
(24.1g saturated fat); 1994kJ
(477 cal); 27.1g carbohydrate;
5.7g protein; 8.5g fibre

¾ cup (180ml) thickened cream
2 tablespoons icing sugar
200g crème fraîche
250g strawberries, quartered
2 medium bananas (400g), sliced thickly
½ cup (125ml) passionfruit pulp
50g meringue, chopped coarsely
3 medium kiwi fruit (255g), chopped coarsely

You need 6 passionfruit to get the required amount of pulp for this recipe. Packaged pavlova "nests" and meringues can be found at your supermarket.

1 Beat cream and icing sugar in small bowl with electric mixer until soft peaks form; stir in crème fraîche.
2 Divide strawberries and banana among four 1½-cup (375ml) glasses. Top with half the passionfruit pulp.
3 Divide crème fraîche mixture among glasses; top with meringue, kiwi fruit and remaining passionfruit pulp.

easy desserts

grilled pineapple with coconut ice-cream

The day before, fold 1 cup toasted shredded coconut and ¼ cup Malibu into 1-litre softened vanilla ice-cream; freeze, covered, overnight. The next night, combine 1 tablespoon Malibu and 2 tablespoons brown sugar in large bowl; add 1 thickly sliced large pineapple, toss to coat in sugar mixture. Brown pineapple, both sides, on heated oiled grill plate; serve with coconut ice-cream.
serves 4 per serving 26g total fat (19.8g saturated fat); 2128kJ (509 cal); 49.4g carbohydrate; 7.7g protein; 7.3g fibre

peach and amaretti crumbles

Preheat oven to 200°C/180°C fan-forced. Grease four 1¼-cup ovenproof dishes. Cook 4 thickly sliced large peaches, 2 tablespoons caster sugar and ½ teaspoon mixed spice in medium saucepan, over medium heat, until peaches are tender; divide mixture among dishes. Meanwhile, combine 125g crushed amaretti biscuits, ¼ cup almond meal and ¼ cup plain flour in medium bowl; rub in 80g chopped butter then sprinkle mixture evenly over peaches. Place dishes on oven tray; cook, uncovered, about 15 minutes or until browned.
serves 4 per serving 28.4g total fat (16.8g saturated fat); 1889kJ (452 cal); 42.5g carbohydrate; 5.3g protein; 5.6g fibre

strawberries and mint in orange syrup

Stir ¼ cup water and 2 tablespoons grated palm sugar in small saucepan, over low heat, until sugar dissolves; bring to a boil. Boil, uncovered, without stirring, about 3 minutes or until syrup thickens slightly. Remove from heat; stir in 2 teaspoons finely grated orange rind and 2 tablespoons orange juice; cool. Combine 500g quartered strawberries and ¼ cup coarsely chopped fresh mint in medium bowl with syrup. Divide mixture among bowls; serve with ⅔ cup crème fraîche.
serves 4 per serving 15.2g total fat (9.9g saturated fat); 840kJ (201 cal); 11.8g carbohydrate; 3.2g protein; 3.1g fibre

mixed berry and mascarpone brioche bruschetta

Using an electric mixer, beat 300ml cream and 1 tablespoon icing sugar in small bowl until soft peaks form; fold in 250g mascarpone. Toast 6 thick slices brioche; place one on each serving plate, spread with mascarpone mixture; top with combined 150g raspberries and 150g blueberries. Sprinkle with a little finely chopped fresh mint.
serves 6 per serving 47.6g total fat (29.8g saturated fat); 2725kJ (652 cal); 46.4g carbohydrate; 9.9g protein; 3.3g fibre

passionfruit and banana fool

The day before, divide 6 coarsely chopped sponge-finger biscuits among six 1-cup parfait glasses; drizzle ½ cup tropical fruit juice equally over biscuits in glasses. Beat 300ml cream in small bowl with electric mixer until soft peaks form; fold in 1 cup vanilla yogurt and ½ cup passionfruit pulp; spoon half the mixture into glasses, top with 2 thinly sliced small bananas then remaining mixture. Drizzle 2 more tablespoons passionfruit pulp over each fool. Refrigerate, covered, overnight.
serves 6 per serving 20.4g total fat (13.3g saturated fat); 1271kJ (304 cal); 22.4g carbohydrate; 5.4g protein; 3.7g fibre

grilled pineapple with coconut ice-cream

peach and amaretti crumbles

strawberries and mint in orange syrup

mixed berry and mascarpone brioche bruschetta

passionfruit and banana fool

drinks

pineapple, orange and passionfruit frappé

Strain ½ cup passionfruit pulp through sieve into small bowl; reserve seeds and liquid. Blend or process 1 coarsely chopped medium pineapple, ¾ cup fresh orange juice and reserved passionfruit liquid, in batches, until smooth. Add 1 teaspoon finely grated orange rind and 2 cups crushed ice; pulse until combined. Stir in seeds.

makes 1.5 litres (6 cups)

per cup 0.2g total fat (0g saturated fat); 284kJ (68 cal); 11.6g carbohydrate; 1.8g protein; 5g fibre

tropical punch

Combine 1 coarsely chopped medium mango, 200g finely chopped pineapple, 250g thinly sliced strawberries, 3 cups chilled pineapple juice, 1½ cups chilled dry ginger ale, ½ cup orange juice, ⅓ cup lime juice, ⅓ cup Malibu, ⅓ cup vodka and 2 tablespoons finely shredded fresh mint leaves in large jug. Serve over crushed ice.

makes 2 litres (8 cups)

per cup 0.3g total fat (0g saturated fat); 619kJ (418 cal); 23.2g carbohydrate; 1.6g protein; 1.9g fibre

beetroot, rocket and orange juice

Push 350g coarsely chopped raw beetroot, 6 coarsely chopped medium oranges and 80g rocket leaves through juice extractor. Stir in ⅔ cup water and 1 teaspoon finely grated orange rind.

makes 1 litre (4 cups)

per cup 0.4g total fat (0g saturated fat); 543kJ (130 cal); 23.8g carbohydrate; 4.4g protein; 7g fibre

raspberry mint iced tea

Combine 2 tablespoons caster sugar and 2 cups hot water in large heatproof jug; stir until sugar dissolves. Add 6 raspberry tea bags; stand 10 minutes. Add ⅓ cup fresh raspberries, 1 cup coarsely chopped fresh mint and 2 cups chilled water. Cover, refrigerate 20 minutes; remove tea bags. Serve over crushed ice.

makes 1 litre (4 cups)

per cup 0.2g total fat (0g saturated fat); 180kJ (43 cal); 9.5g carbohydrate; 0.5g protein; 1.4g fibre

strawberry and cranberry spritzer

Push 300g thawed frozen cranberries and 400g hulled strawberries through juice extractor. Stir in 8 shredded large fresh mint leaves, 100g thinly sliced strawberries and 3½ cups chilled soda water. Serve over crushed ice.

makes 1.5 litres (6 cups)

per cup 0.2g total fat (0g saturated fat); 151kJ (36 cal); 4.2g carbohydrate; 1.6g protein; 2.8g fibre

pineapple, orange and passionfruit frappé

tropical punch

beetroot, rocket and orange juice

raspberry mint iced tea

strawberry and cranberry spritzer

glossary

ALMONDS flat, pointy-tipped nuts having a pitted brown shell enclosing a creamy white kernel covered by a brown skin.

slivered lengthways-cut pieces.

AMARETTI BISCUITS Italian almond-flavoured biscuits; shaped like a small dome, they have a light, crunchy texture.

BOCCONCINI walnut-sized, baby mozzarella; a delicate, semi-soft, white cheese traditionally made from buffalo milk. Sold fresh, it spoils rapidly so will only keep, refrigerated in brine, for one or two days at the most.

BROCCOLINI a cross between broccoli and chinese kale; has long asparagus-like stems with a long loose floret, both of which are edible. Resembles broccoli in look, but is milder and sweeter.

CANNELLINI BEANS a small white bean similar in appearance and flavour to great northern, navy and haricot beans. Available dried or canned.

CAPERS the grey-green buds of a warm climate (usually Mediterranean) shrub, sold either dried and salted or pickled in a vinegar brine. Tiny young baby capers are also available both in brine or dried in salt. Rinse well before using.

CAPSICUM also known as pepper or bell pepper. Native to Central and South America; found in red, green, yellow, orange and purplish-black varieties. Seeds and membranes should be discarded before use.

CARAWAY SEEDS small, half-moon-shaped dried seed from a member of the parsley family; adds a sharp anise flavour when used in both sweet and savoury dishes.

CHERVIL also known as cicily; mildly fennel-flavoured member of the parsley family with curly dark-green leaves. Available both fresh and dried.

CHICKPEAS also called channa, garbanzos or hummus; a sandy-coloured, irregularly round legume available canned or dried (the latter need several hours reconstituting in cold water before being used).

CHINESE COOKING WINE also known as hao hsing or chinese rice wine; made from fermented rice, wheat, sugar and salt with a 13.5 per cent alcohol content. Found in Asian food shops; if you can't find it, replace with mirin or sherry.

CHORIZO sausage of Spanish origin; made of coarsely ground pork and highly seasoned with garlic and chilli.

CORIANDER also known as pak chee, cilantro or chinese parsley; a bright-green-leafed herb having both pungent aroma and taste. The stems and roots of the herb are also used in Thai cooking; wash well before chopping. Also available ground or as seeds; these should not be substituted for fresh coriander as the tastes are completely different.

CORN, BABY pale-yellow cobs of corn that are harvested while still young and tender.

CORNFLOUR also known as cornstarch. Made from corn or wheat and used as a thickening agent in cooking.

CORNMEAL often called polenta, to which this ground corn (maize) is similar, albeit coarser. One can be substituted for the other, but textures will vary.

COUSCOUS a fine, grain-like cereal product made from semolina; it is rehydrated by steaming or with the addition of a warm liquid, and swells to three or four times its original size.

CREME FRAICHE a mature, naturally fermented cream having a velvety texture and slightly tangy, nutty flavour.

CUMIN also known as zeera or comino; available dried as seeds or ground.

CURRANTS, DRIED tiny, almost black, raisins.

FENNEL also known as finocchio or anise; also the name given to the dried seeds, which have a stronger licorice flavour.

FRIED SHALLOTS served on Asian tables as a condiment to be sprinkled over just-cooked food. Found in cellophane bags or jars at Asian grocery shops; once opened, they will keep for months if stored tightly seeled.

GOLDEN SYRUP a by-product of refined sugarcane; honey or pure maple syrup can be substituted.

HUMMUS a Middle Eastern salad or dip made from softened dried chickpeas, garlic, lemon juice and tahini (sesame seed paste); can be purchased ready-made from delicatessens and supermarkets.

KAFFIR LIME LEAVES also known as bai magrood; look like two glossy dark-green leaves joined end to end, forming a rounded hourglass shape. A strip of fresh lime peel may be substituted for each kaffir lime leaf.

KECAP ASIN, KECAP MANIS *see sauces*.

KIPFLER small, finger-shaped, knobbly potato with nutty flavour.

KUMARA the Polynesian name of an orange-fleshed sweet potato.

LAMB
backstrap also known as eye of loin; the tender, larger fillet from a row of loin chops or cutlets.
french-trimmed cutlets small, tender rib chop with all the fat and gristle at the narrow end of the bone removed.

LEMON THYME LEAVES a member of the mint family; its scent is due to the high level of citral in its leaves, an oil also found in lemon, orange, verbena and lemon grass. The citrus scent is enhanced by crushing the leaves before using.

MALIBU a white Caribbean rum, flavoured with coconut.

MAPLE SYRUP distilled from the sap of sugar-maple trees. Maple-flavoured syrup or pancake syrup is not an adequate substitute for the real thing.

MINCE also known as ground, as in ground beef, veal, lamb, pork or chicken.

MINUTE STEAKS boneless cuts of beef from the tender muscle running from rump to ankle.

MIRIN a Japanese champagne-coloured cooking wine, made of glutinous rice and alcohol. It is used expressly for cooking and should not be confused with sake.

MUSHROOMS
dried shitake also known as donko or dried chinese mushrooms; have a unique meaty flavour. Rehydrate before use.
oyster also known as abalone; grey-white mushrooms shaped like a fan. Have a smooth texture and a subtle, oyster-like, flavour.

swiss brown also known as roman or cremini. Light- to dark-brown mushrooms with a full-bodied flavour.

NEW-YORK CUT STEAKS boneless beef striploin steak.

NOODLES
hokkien also known as stir-fry noodles; fresh wheat noodles resembling thick, yellow-brown spaghetti needing no pre-cooking before use.
singapore pre-cooked fresh wheat noodles best described as a thinner version of hokkien.
soba thin Japanese noodles made from a mix of buckwheat flour and wheat flour.

OIL
peanut pressed from ground peanuts; the most commonly used oil in Asian cooking because of its high smoke point (capacity to handle high heat without burning).
sesame made from roasted, crushed, white sesame seeds; most often used as a flavouring rather than a cooking medium.
vegetable sourced from plants rather than animal fats.

PANCETTA an Italian unsmoked bacon. Pork belly is cured in salt and spices then rolled into a sausage shape and dried.

PEPITAS the pale green kernels of dried pumpkin seeds; they can be bought plain or salted.

PITTA also known as lebanese bread; wheat-flour pocket bread sold in large, flat pieces that separate into two thin rounds. Also available in small thick pieces called pocket pitta.

PLAIN FLOUR an all-purpose flour made from wheat.

POLENTA also known as cornmeal; a flour-like cereal made of dried corn (maize). Also the name of the dish made from it.

PORK
cutlets cut from the ribs.
fillet skinless, boneless eye-fillet cut from the loin.

PROSCIUTTO a kind of unsmoked Italian ham; salted, air-cured and aged.

OAK-LEAF LETTUCE also known as feuille de chene; curly-leafed but not as frizzy as the coral lettuce. Found in both red and green varieties.

RICOTTA a soft, sweet, moist, white, cow-milk cheese with a low-fat content and a slightly grainy texture. The name roughly translates as "cooked again" and refers to ricotta's manufacture from a whey that is itself a by-product of other cheese making.

ROCKET also known as arugula, rugula and rucola; peppery green leaf eaten raw in salads or used in cooking. Baby rocket leaves are smaller and less peppery.

SALT unless specified otherwise, we use normal iodised table salt. Because we believe cooks salt as they like or not at all, the vast majority of our recipes do not list it as one of the ingredients.

SAMBAL OELEK (also spelled ulek or olek) Indonesian in origin; a salty paste made from ground chillies and vinegar.

SAUCES
barbecue spicy, tomato-based sauce used to marinate, baste or as an accompaniment.
black bean an Asian cooking sauce made from salted and fermented soybeans, spices and wheat flour.

char siu also known as chinese barbecue sauce; a paste-like ingredient made from sugar, water, salt, fermented soybean paste, honey, soy sauce, malt syrup and spices. Available from most supermarkets and Asian food stores.

fish also called naam pla or nuoc naam. Made from pulverised salted fermented fish (most often anchovies); has a pungent smell and strong taste, so use according to your taste.

hoisin a thick, sweet and spicy chinese barbecue sauce made from salted fermented soybeans, onions and garlic. Available from Asian food shops and most supermarkets.

kecap asin a very salty, dark soy sauce from Indonesia.

kecap manis a dark, thick sweet soy sauce with added sweetness derived from the addition of either molasses or palm sugar when brewed.

pasta sauce, bottled a prepared sauce made of a blend of tomatoes, herbs and spices.

soy also known as sieu; made from fermented soybeans. There are several variations available in supermarkets and Asian food stores. *Japanese soy sauce* is an all-purpose low-sodium sauce made with more wheat content than its Chinese counterparts. *Light soy sauce* is fairly thin in consistency and, while paler than the others, is the saltiest tasting; it should not be confused with salt-reduced or low-sodium soy sauces.

worcestershire thin, dark-brown spicy sauce developed by the British when in India; used as a seasoning for meat, gravies and cocktails, and as a condiment.

snake beans long (about 40cm), thin, round, fresh green beans, similar to green or french beans. Also known as yard-long beans.

SUGAR

caster also known as superfine or finely granulated table sugar.

icing also known as powdered sugar or confectioners' sugar; pulverised granulated sugar crushed together with a small amount of cornflour added.

palm also known as jaggery, nam tan pip, jawa or gula melaka; made from the sap of the sugar palm tree. Light brown to black in colour and usually sold in rock-hard cakes; substitute with brown sugar, if unavailable.

raw brown granulated sugar.

white granulated table sugar also known as crystal sugar.

SUMAC a purple-red, astringent spice ground from berries that grow on shrubs that flourish wild around the Mediterranean; has a tart, lemony flavour. Found in Middle-Eastern food stores. *Substitute*: ⅛ teaspoon five-spice *plus* ½ teaspoon lemon pepper *plus* ⅛ teaspoon all spice *equals* ¾ teaspoon sumac.

THAI BASIL also known as horapa; different from holy basil and sweet basil in both look and taste, having smaller leaves and purplish stems. It has a slight aniseed flavour.

TOFU also known as soybean curd or bean curd; an off-white, custard-like product made from the "milk" of crushed soybeans. Comes fresh as soft or firm, and processed as fried or pressed dried sheets. Fresh tofu can be refrigerated in water (changed daily) for up to four days.

TOMATOES

cherry also known as tiny tim or tom thumb tomatoes; small, round tomatoes.

egg also called plum or roma; are smallish and oval-shaped. Much used in Italian cooking.

truss small, vine-ripened tomatoes that still have the vine attached.

VEAL SCHNITZEL thinly sliced steak available crumbed or plain; we used plain schnitzel in our recipes.

VINEGAR

balsamic originally from Modena, Italy, there are now many balsamic vinegars on the market ranging in pungency and quality depending on how, and for how long, they have been aged; use the most expensive sparingly.

cider made from fermented apples.

malt made from fermented malt and beech shavings.

red wine made from red wine.

white wine made from white wine.

WASABI an Asian horseradish used to make the pungent, green-coloured sauce traditionally served with Japanese raw fish dishes; sold in powdered or paste form.

WITLOF also known as belgian endive; related to, and confused with, chicory. Grown in darkness, like white asparagus, to prevent it becoming green; it has tightly furled, cream to light-green leaves and a delicately bitter flavour.

ZUCCHINI also known as courgette; a small, pale- or dark-green, yellow or white vegetable belonging to the squash family. Harvested when young, its edible flowers can be stuffed with a mild cheese or other delicate ingredients then deep-fried or oven-baked.

conversion chart

measures

One Australian metric measuring cup holds approximately 250ml; one Australian metric tablespoon holds 20ml; one Australian metric teaspoon holds 5ml.

The difference between one country's measuring cups and another's is within a two- or three-teaspoon variance, and will not affect your cooking results. North America, New Zealand and the United Kingdom use a 15ml tablespoon.

All cup and spoon measurements are level. The most accurate way of measuring dry ingredients is to weigh them. When measuring liquids, use a clear glass or plastic jug with the metric markings.

We use large eggs with an average weight of 60g.

dry measures

metric	imperial
15g	½oz
30g	1oz
60g	2oz
90g	3oz
125g	4oz (¼lb)
155g	5oz
185g	6oz
220g	7oz
250g	8oz (½lb)
280g	9oz
315g	10oz
345g	11oz
375g	12oz (¾lb)
410g	13oz
440g	14oz
470g	15oz
500g	16oz (1lb)
750g	24oz (1½lb)
1kg	32oz (2lb)

liquid measures

metric	imperial
30ml	1 fluid oz
60ml	2 fluid oz
100ml	3 fluid oz
125ml	4 fluid oz
150ml	5 fluid oz (¼ pint/1 gill)
190ml	6 fluid oz
250ml	8 fluid oz
300ml	10 fluid oz (½ pint)
500ml	16 fluid oz
600ml	20 fluid oz (1 pint)
1000ml (1 litre)	1¾ pints

length measures

metric	imperial
3mm	⅛in
6mm	¼in
1cm	½in
2cm	¾in
2.5cm	1in
5cm	2in
6cm	2½in
8cm	3in
10cm	4in
13cm	5in
15cm	6in
18cm	7in
20cm	8in
23cm	9in
25cm	10in
28cm	11in
30cm	12in (1ft)

oven temperatures

These oven temperatures are only a guide for conventional ovens. For fan-forced ovens, check the manufacturer's manual.

	°C (Celsius)	°F (Fahrenheit)	Gas Mark
Very slow	120	250	½
Slow	150	275-300	1-2
Moderately slow	160	325	3
Moderate	180	350-375	4-5
Moderately hot	200	400	6
Hot	220	425-450	7-8
Very hot	240	475	9

index

ARE YOU MISSING SOME OF THE WORLD'S FAVOURITE COOKBOOKS?

The Australian Women's Weekly Cookbooks are available from bookshops, cookshops, supermarkets and other stores all over the world. You can also buy direct from the publisher, using the order form below.

TITLE	RRP	QTY	TITLE	RRP	QTY
Asian, Meals in Minutes	£6.99		Indian Cooking Class	£6.99	
Babies & Toddlers Good Food	£6.99		Japanese Cooking Class	£6.99	
Barbecue Meals In Minutes	£6.99		Just For One (Feb 07)	£6.99	
Beginners Cooking Class	£6.99		Kids' Birthday Cakes	£6.99	
Beginners Simple Meals	£6.99		Kids Cooking	£6.99	
Beginners Thai	£6.99		Kids' Cooking Step-by-Step	£6.99	
Best Food	£6.99		Lean Food	£6.99	
Best Food Desserts	£6.99		Low-carb, Low-fat	£6.99	
Best Food Fast	£6.99		Low-fat Feasts	£6.99	
Best Food Mains	£6.99		Low-fat Food For Life	£6.99	
Cafe Classics	£6.99		Low-fat Meals in Minutes	£6.99	
Cakes Biscuits & Slices	£6.99		Main Course Salads	£6.99	
Cakes Cooking Class	£6.99		Mexican	£6.99	
Caribbean Cooking	£6.99		Middle Eastern Cooking Class	£6.99	
Casseroles	£6.99		Midweek Meals in Minutes	£6.99	
Casseroles & Slow-Cooked Classics	£6.99		Moroccan & the Foods of North Africa	£6.99	
Cheap Eats (Feb 07)	£6.99		Muffins, Scones & Breads	£6.99	
Cheesecakes: baked and chilled	£6.99		New Casseroles	£6.99	
Chicken	£6.99		New Classics	£6.99	
Chicken Meals in Minutes	£6.99		New Curries	£6.99	
Chinese Cooking Class	£6.99		New Finger Food	£6.99	
Christmas Cooking	£6.99		New Salads	£6.99	
Chocolate	£6.99		Party Food and Drink	£6.99	
Cocktails	£6.99		Pasta Meals in Minutes	£6.99	
Cooking for Friends	£6.99		Potatoes	£6.99	
Cupcakes & Fairycakes	£6.99		Salads: Simple, Fast & Fresh	£6.99	
Detox	£6.99		Saucery	£6.99	
Dinner Beef	£6.99		Sauces Salsas & Dressings	£6.99	
Dinner Lamb	£6.99		Sensational Stir-Fries	£6.99	
Dinner Seafood	£6.99		Slim	£6.99	
Easy Curry	£6.99		Stir-fry	£6.99	
Easy Spanish-Style	£6.99		Superfoods for Exam Success	£6.99	
Essential Soup	£6.99		Sweet Old Fashioned Favourites	£6.99	
Foods That Fight Back	£6.99		Tapas Mezze Antipasto & other bites	£6.99	
French Food, New	£6.99		Thai Cooking Class	£6.99	
Fresh Food Fast	£6.99		Traditional Italian	£6.99	
Fresh Food for Babies & Toddlers	£6.99		Vegetarian Meals in Minutes	£6.99	
Good Food Fast	£6.99		Vegie Food	£6.99	
Great Lamb Cookbook	£6.99		Wicked Sweet Indulgences	£6.99	
Greek Cooking Class	£6.99		Wok, Meals in Minutes	£6.99	
Grills	£6.99				
Healthy Heart Cookbook	£6.99		TOTAL COST:	£	

Mr/Mrs/Ms _____

Address _____

_____ Postcode _____

Day time phone _____ Email* (optional) _____

I enclose my cheque/money order for £ _____

or please charge £ _____

to my: ☐ Access ☐ Mastercard ☐ Visa ☐ Diners Club

PLEASE NOTE: WE DO NOT ACCEPT SWITCH OR ELECTRON CARDS

Card number [ ][ ][ ][ ] [ ][ ][ ][ ] [ ][ ][ ][ ] [ ][ ][ ][ ]

Expiry date _____ 3 digit security code *(found on reverse of card)* _____

Cardholder's name_____ Signature _____

To order: Mail or fax – photocopy or complete the order form above, and send your credit card details or cheque payable to: Australian Consolidated Press (UK), Moulton Park Business Centre, Red House Road, Moulton Park, Northampton NN3 6AQ, phone (+44) (0) 1604 497531 fax (+44) (0) 1604 497533, e-mail books@acpuk.com or order online at www.acpuk.com

Non-UK residents: We accept the credit cards listed on the coupon, or cheques, drafts or International Money Orders payable in sterling and drawn on a UK bank. Credit card charges are at the exchange rate current at the time of payment.

Postage and packing UK: Add £1.00 per order plus 50p per book.

Postage and packing overseas: Add £2.00 per order plus £1.00 per book.

All pricing current at time of going to press and subject to change/availability.

Offer ends 31.12.2007

* By including your email address, you consent to receipt of any email regarding this magazine, and other emails which inform you of ACP's other publications, products, services and events, and to promote third party goods and services in which you may be interested.